The Gratitude Journal

The cover art, caricature images, and quotes with images in this journal were created by the author and she owns and retains all rights to them.

This Journal Belongs to

_____

Welcome to Your Ennobling Journey!

We do not enter this world alone, and we do not exit this world alone. We have help from our mother and strangers to make our entrance, literally kicking and screaming. Others carry us to our final resting place, be it a burial or cremation. **If our entry into this life and exit from this life are assisted processes, why do we convince ourselves that everything in between is a solo pursuit?**

Once we accept the reality that we need to build relationships with others to pursue our purpose, we can balance our individuality with the need to lean into others to be supported. The trick to having a support system that facilitates our pursuits is to be the support system for others. Can you go to the ATM and withdraw money when you need it if you never invested the time to select a bank, establish a relationship, open an account, and deposit funds? Life itself is a bank account. We can each only withdraw what we have deposited.

To build human relationships necessary to sustain us, we need to be kind, caring, compassionate, and empathetic. We must also have the humility to learn from our experiences and navigate life's challenges with grace. We invest these noble qualities into our relationships to build our support system account. This is not a monetary account in a financial bank; it is an ennobling account in a heart bank. **We are each a constant gardener of our journey to success where our authentic relationships become the wondrous flowers bearing fruitful results. Gratitude is a magical fertilizer that helps us cultivate that blossoming garden.** I have created the journal cover image to visually represent this message of being a constant gardener to let it speak and capture your imagination. I hope that the imagery evokes in you the desire to become the gardener of your destiny.

In my international bestseller, *Ennobled for Success: From Civil War to a US CFO*, I take you through the journey to acquire the noble qualities of kindness, care, compassion, and empathy to develop into the *being* who welcomes life with humility and grace. Gratitude is the conduit for acquiring these noble qualities. Therefore, when we connect with our *being* and channel it to influence all we are *doing*, rooted in a sense of gratitude, we create the opportunity to build authentic relationships that facilitate our success by converting each roadblock into stepping stones for success.

Keeping a gratitude journal has been an important part of my journey since childhood. It anchored me and gave me the context I needed as a child in a warzone and shaped me into adulthood. Embracing life lessons, having the humility to learn from fellow travelers no matter who they are, facing challenges head-on with grace, and staying grateful regardless of the underlying nature of situations were key to finding my balance in life to becoming ennobled. The gratitude journal helped me remain vulnerable enough to allow others into my life and transform me into a better version of myself. The more grateful I felt, the more I could handle my anger, fear, sadness, and other negative emotions swirling within me. I started becoming curious as to why. As I grew older and was introduced to biology and sciences as a teenager, I started learning how the sense of gratitude truly influenced brain chemistry and gave me a superpower to thrive despite my circumstances. Being a visual thinker, I had the image in my mind, based on my readings, how gratitude helped me rewire my brain function. Over the years, that visualization has been refined. I share my visualization here with the intent to help you benefit from my learnings. (1)

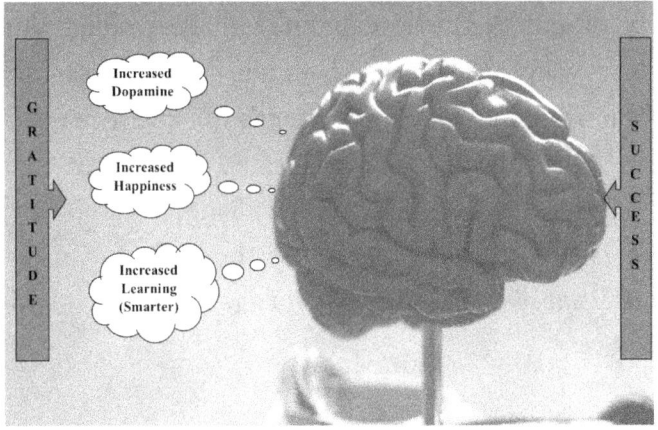

Adapted from *Psychology Today*, Dr. Kasthuri Henry, © *Ennobled for Success*

This Gratitude Journal is meant to accompany *Ennobled for Success: From Civil War to a US CFO*, as a fifty-two-week reflective exercise to help facilitate your transformational journey, so you have the opportunity to adopt this ennobling road for your success. I have enjoyed creating the fifty-two images of my younger self and integrating my motivational quotes to set the tone for your weekly journey embracing positive brain chemistry. The journal contains the opportunity to capture:

1. The week's experience
    a. What Happened
    b. How It Impacted Me
    c. Why I Am Grateful
2. The Week's Self Reflection

With heartfelt gratitude to all those who have touched my life, I introduce you to the *Gratitude Journal*. As you begin your journey of gratitude, please keep an open mind, become aware of your surroundings, develop the ability to see with your heart, and build the courage to be vulnerable enough to let strangers in. My life has taught me that a rickshaw driver in a war-torn country can teach a scared and angry little girl the value of listening to giving a person their voice. A sixth-grade Catholic nun can teach a little Hindu girl to unapologetically embrace kindness with courage and turn it into a superpower. An entire community of Indian slums and rural villagers could care enough to embrace that lonely teenager to teach her the joy of servant leadership. Strangers can walk into a young woman's life and teach her how to trust and build relationships that stand the test of time and distance. All this is possible only when we allow it to happen by being vulnerable. **Ennobling is not the prerogative of the rich and affluent. It is a selfless gift that comes from a courageous heart of kindness and compassion.**

Step into your purpose. Embrace a life of being ennobled. As you take charge of your destiny and navigate toward your success, maintain perspective, and find your inner joy. Keep the faith that **the universe will rise to meet you because it is perfectly in tune with the energy you create around you.**

Letter to the Reader

Dear Fellow Traveler,

As you embark on the journey within to connect with your inner-self, I take this opportunity to wish you a fulfilling experience! I wrote *Ennobled for Success: From Civil War to a US CFO* to help you *discover wisdom-filled lessons to support you in living an ennobled, empowered, and positive life.* I then brought forward this *Gratitude Journal* to help facilitate your ennobling process.

Your life well lived will be the message you leave behind as your legacy. How you live your purpose and light up the spark in others is your secret to building that legacy. This is the beginning of that process. Put aside anything anyone has ever said to you about what you are not and what you cannot be. **You are enough! You are a magical mix of who you are meant to be in your unique way.** Stay open to finding yourself, making peace within, and then drawing from what you build inside of you to shape your path forward. Join our Ennobled For Success Facebook group to be surrounded by other travelers who seek this same path to find a support system that will hold space for you.

Remember, the universe will rise to meet you as you transform and emanate the positive energy that maintains harmony. Every human interaction and every human exploration are your opportunities for your transformation. So, embrace your transformation with abandon and live your purposeful life with courageous optimism.

Warm Wishes,

Kasthuri Henry

Dr. Kasthuri Henry, PhD, CTP

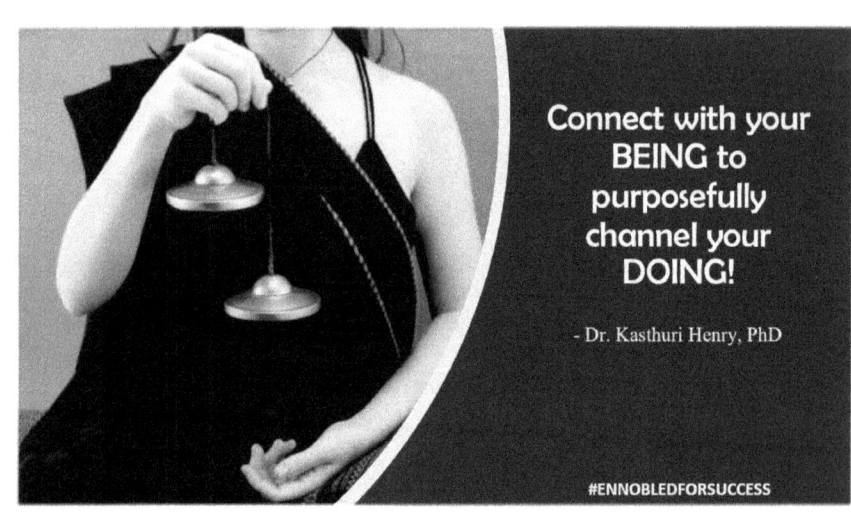

Weekly Reflection

Week ___

What happened this week?

How does this impact me?

Why am I grateful?

Weekly insight/reflection:

_____
_____
_____
_____
_____
_____

Weekly Reflection

Week ___

What happened this week?

How does this impact me?

Why am I grateful?

Weekly insight/reflection:

_____
_____
_____
_____
_____
_____

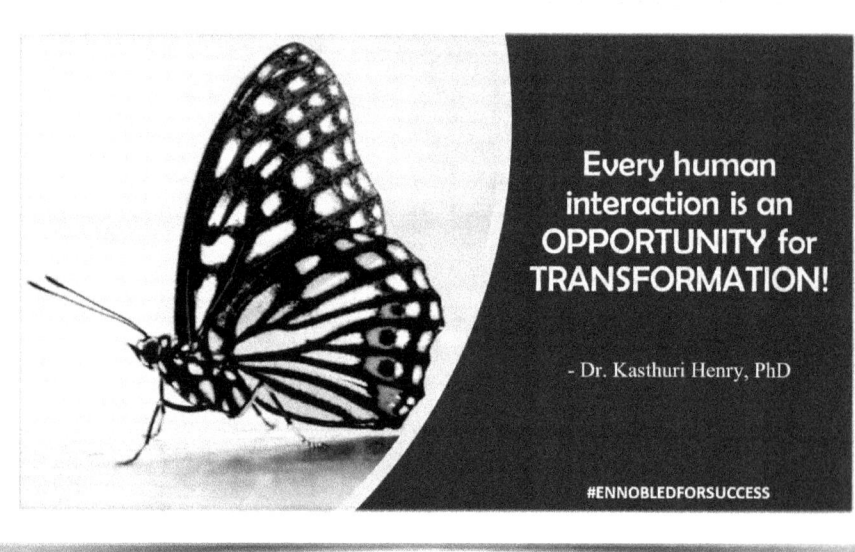

Weekly Reflection

Week ___

What happened this week?

How does this impact me?

Why am I grateful?

Weekly insight/reflection:

_____
_____
_____
_____
_____
_____

Weekly Reflection

Week ___

What happened this week?

How does this impact me?

Why am I grateful?

Weekly insight/reflection:

_____
_____
_____
_____
_____
_____

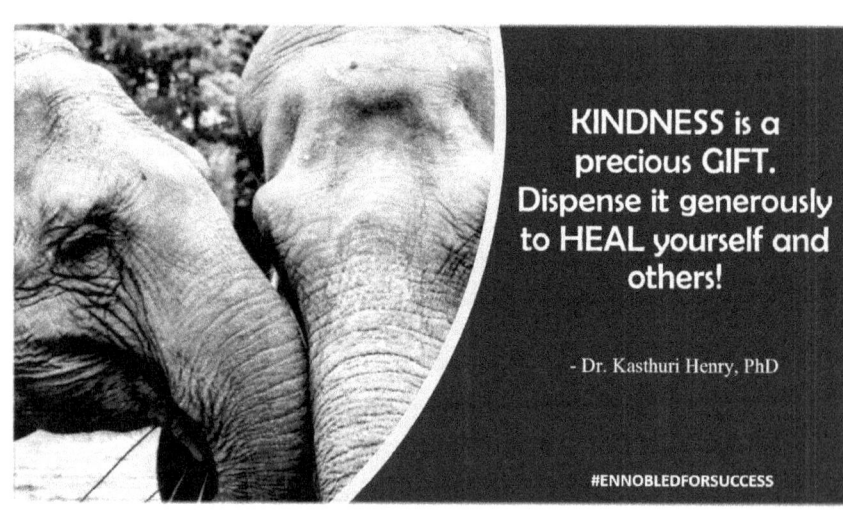

Weekly Reflection

Week ___

What happened this week?

How does this impact me?

Why am I grateful?

Weekly insight/reflection:

_____

_____

_____

_____

_____

_____

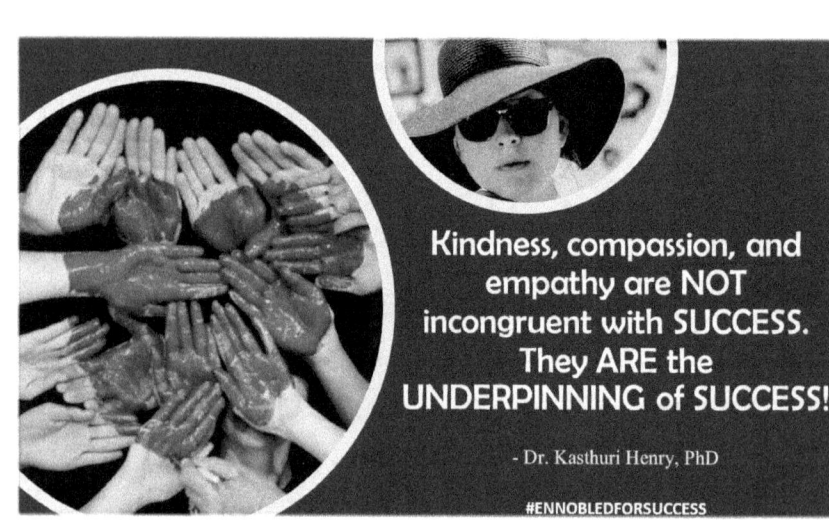

Weekly Reflection

Week ___

What happened this week?

How does this impact me?

Why am I grateful?

Weekly insight/reflection:

_____
_____
_____
_____
_____

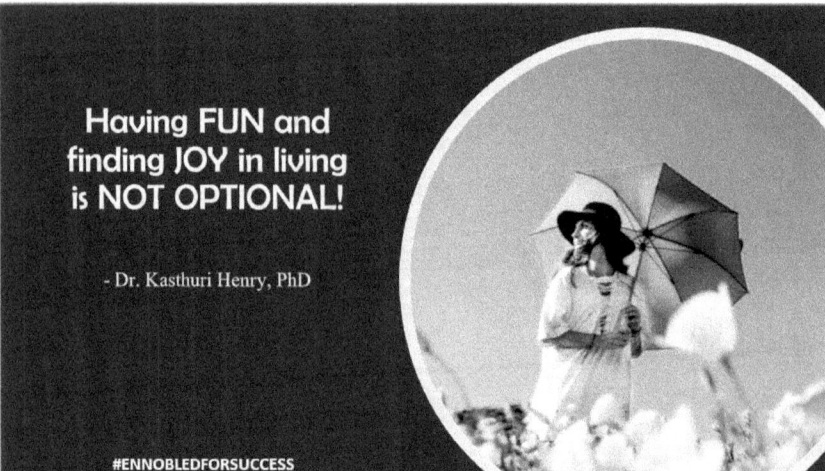

Weekly Reflection

Week ___

What happened this week?

How does this impact me?

Why am I grateful?

Weekly insight/reflection:

_____
_____
_____
_____
_____
_____

Weekly Reflection

Week ___

What happened this week?

How does this impact me?

Why am I grateful?

Weekly insight/reflection:

_____
_____
_____
_____
_____
_____

Weekly Reflection

Week ___

What happened this week?

How does this impact me?

Why am I grateful?

Weekly insight/reflection:

_____

_____

_____

_____

_____

_____

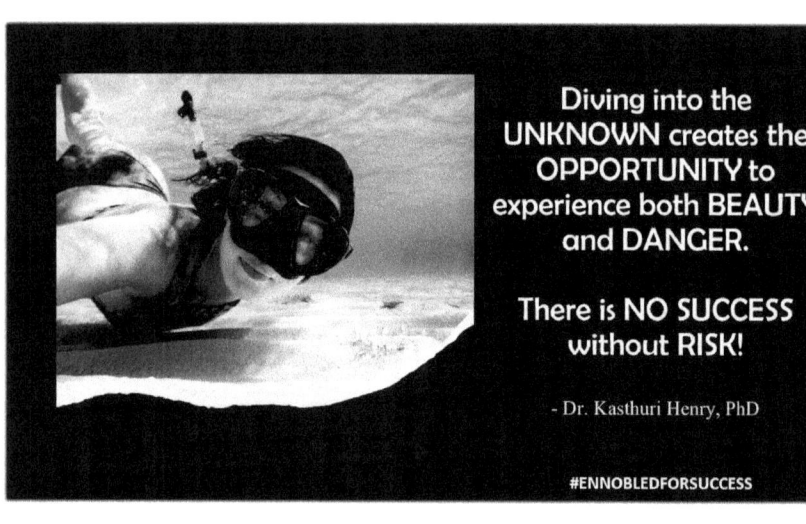

Weekly Reflection

Week ___

What happened this week?

How does this impact me?

Why am I grateful?

Weekly insight/reflection:

_____
_____
_____
_____
_____
_____

Weekly Reflection

Week ___

What happened this week?

How does this impact me?

Why am I grateful?

Weekly insight/reflection:

_____
_____
_____
_____
_____
_____

Weekly Reflection

Week ___

What happened this week?

How does this impact me?

Why am I grateful?

Weekly insight/reflection:

_____
_____
_____
_____
_____
_____

The LIGHT in your SOUL lights up your journey.

Dare to SHINE on!

- Dr. Kasthuri Henry, PhD

#ENNOBLEDFORSUCCESS

Weekly Reflection

Week ___

What happened this week?

How does this impact me?

Why am I grateful?

Weekly insight/reflection:

_____
_____
_____
_____
_____
_____

Weekly Reflection   *Week* ___

What happened this week?

How does this impact me?

Why am I grateful?

Weekly insight/reflection:

_____
_____
_____
_____
_____
_____

Learning to TRUST is fundamental to Living with PURPOSE.

Take the leap towards your dream EMPOWERED by TRUST!

- Dr. Kasthuri Henry, PhD

#ENNOBLEDFORSUCCESS

Weekly Reflection

Week ____

What happened this week?

How does this impact me?

Why am I grateful?

Weekly insight/reflection:

_____

_____

_____

_____

_____

_____

Weekly Reflection

Week ___

What happened this week?

How does this impact me?

Why am I grateful?

Weekly insight/reflection:

_____
_____
_____
_____
_____
_____

Weekly Reflection

Week ___

What happened this week?

How does this impact me?

Why am I grateful?

Weekly insight/reflection:

_____

_____

_____

_____

_____

_____

Iron fist in a velvet glove is STRENGTH with VULNERABILITY.

Firm professionalism and kindness is thus a POWER COMBINATION!

- Dr. Kasthuri Henry, PhD

#ENNOBLEDFORSUCCESS

Weekly Reflection

Week ___

What happened this week?

How does this impact me?

Why am I grateful?

Weekly insight/reflection:

_____

_____

_____

_____

_____

_____

Weekly Reflection

Week ___

What happened this week?

How does this impact me?

Why am I grateful?

Weekly insight/reflection:

_____
_____
_____
_____
_____
_____

Weekly Reflection

Week ___

What happened this week?

How does this impact me?

Why am I grateful?

Weekly insight/reflection:
_____
_____
_____
_____
_____

Create your PLAYBOOK.
Shape your PATH.
Live your DESTINY.

- Dr. Kasthuri Henry, PhD

#ENNOBLEDFORSUCCESS

Weekly Reflection

Week ___

What happened this week?

How does this impact me?

Why am I grateful?

Weekly insight/reflection:

_____

_____

_____

_____

_____

_____

BALANCE comes from finding INNER PEACE!

- Dr. Kasthuri Henry, PhD

#ENNOBLEDFORSUCCESS

Weekly Reflection

Week ___

What happened this week?

How does this impact me?

Why am I grateful?

Weekly insight/reflection:

_____
_____
_____
_____
_____
_____

Weekly Reflection

Week ___

What happened this week?

How does this impact me?

Why am I grateful?

Weekly insight/reflection:

_____
_____
_____
_____
_____

Showing up with KINDNES does not cause your inner lion to diminish.

It only makes you more COURAGOUS!

- Dr. Kasthuri Henry, PhD

#ENNOBLEDFORSUCCESS

Weekly Reflection

Week ___

What happened this week?

How does this impact me?

Why am I grateful?

Weekly insight/reflection:

_____
_____
_____
_____
_____
_____

Weekly Reflection

Week ___

What happened this week?

How does this impact me?

Why am I grateful?

Weekly insight/reflection:

_____
_____
_____
_____
_____
_____

Let your SOUL ENKINDLE another!

– Dr. Kasthuri Henry, PhD

#ENNOBLEDFORSUCCESS

Weekly Reflection

Week ___

What happened this week?

How does this impact me?

Why am I grateful?

Weekly insight/reflection:

_____
_____
_____
_____
_____
_____

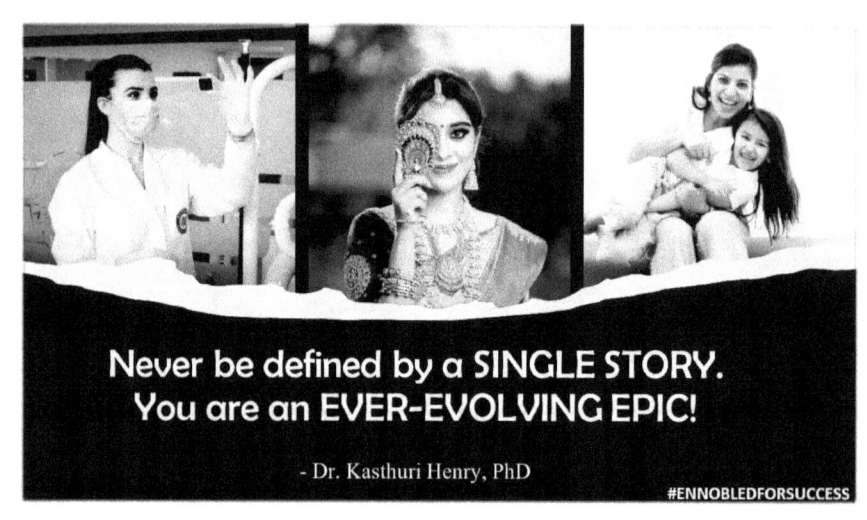

Weekly Reflection

Week ___

What happened this week?

How does this impact me?

Why am I grateful?

Weekly insight/reflection:

_____
_____
_____
_____
_____
_____

Live life in a way to
NOTICE OPPORTUNITY.

Lean in to be a
CATALYST for HEALING!

- Dr. Kasthuri Henry, PhD

#ENNOBLEDFORSUCCESS

Weekly Reflection

Week ___

What happened this week?

How does this impact me?

Why am I grateful?

Weekly insight/reflection:

_____
_____
_____
_____
_____
_____

Weekly Reflection

Week ___

What happened this week?

How does this impact me?

Why am I grateful?

Weekly insight/reflection:

_____
_____
_____
_____
_____
_____

Weekly Reflection

Week ___

What happened this week?

How does this impact me?

Why am I grateful?

Weekly insight/reflection:

_____
_____
_____
_____
_____
_____

Weekly Reflection

Week ___

What happened this week?

How does this impact me?

Why am I grateful?

Weekly insight/reflection:

_____
_____
_____
_____
_____
_____

Weekly Reflection

Week ___

What happened this week?

How does this impact me?

Why am I grateful?

Weekly insight/reflection:

_____
_____
_____
_____
_____
_____

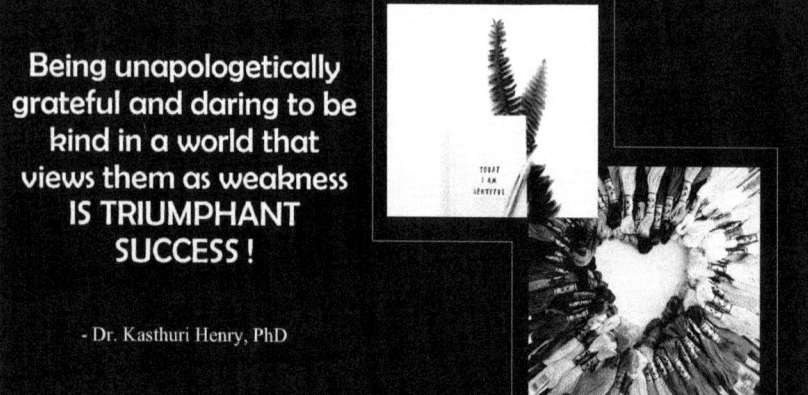

Weekly Reflection

Week ___

What happened this week?

How does this impact me?

Why am I grateful?

Weekly insight/reflection:

_____
_____
_____
_____
_____
_____

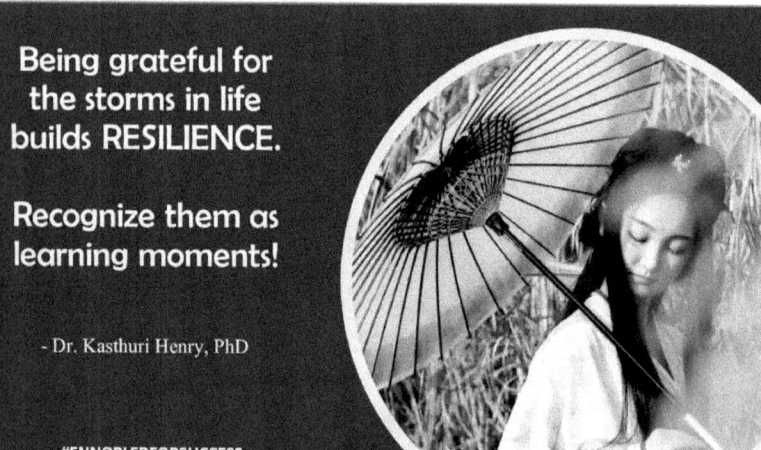

Weekly Reflection

Week ___

What happened this week?

How does this impact me?

Why am I grateful?

Weekly insight/reflection:

_____
_____
_____
_____
_____
_____

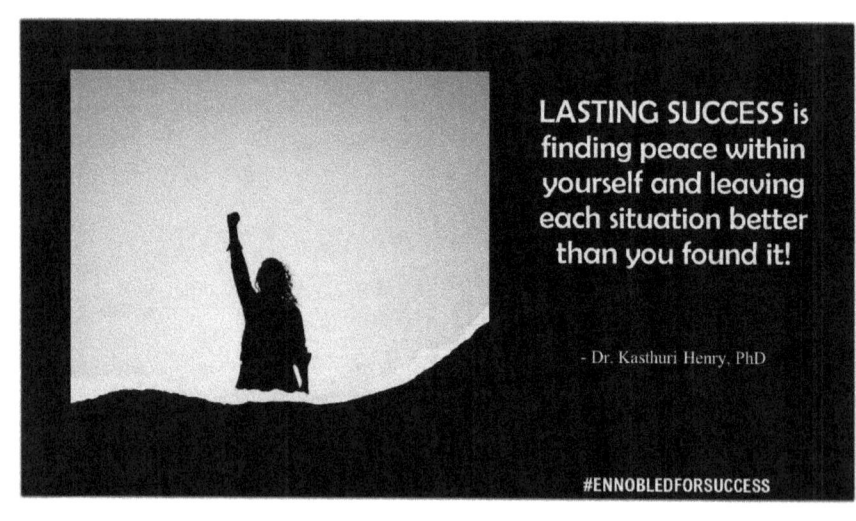

Weekly Reflection

Week ___

What happened this week?

How does this impact me?

Why am I grateful?

Weekly insight/reflection:

_____
_____
_____
_____
_____
_____

Weekly Reflection

Week ___

What happened this week?

How does this impact me?

Why am I grateful?

Weekly insight/reflection:

_____
_____
_____
_____
_____

Weekly Reflection

Week ___

What happened this week?

How does this impact me?

Why am I grateful?

Weekly insight/reflection:

_____
_____
_____
_____
_____
_____

Weekly Reflection

Week ___

What happened this week?

How does this impact me?

Why am I grateful?

Weekly insight/reflection:

_____
_____
_____
_____
_____
_____

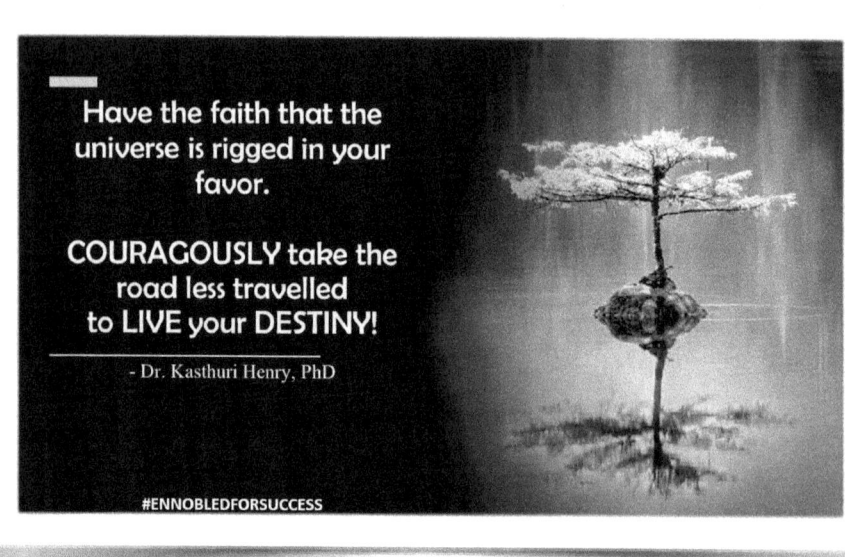

Weekly Reflection

Week ___

What happened this week?

How does this impact me?

Why am I grateful?

Weekly insight/reflection:

_____

_____

_____

_____

_____

_____

Weekly Reflection

Week ___

What happened this week?

How does this impact me?

Why am I grateful?

Weekly insight/reflection:

_____

_____

_____

_____

_____

_____

Weekly Reflection

Week ___

What happened this week?

How does this impact me?

Why am I grateful?

Weekly insight/reflection:

_____
_____
_____
_____
_____
_____

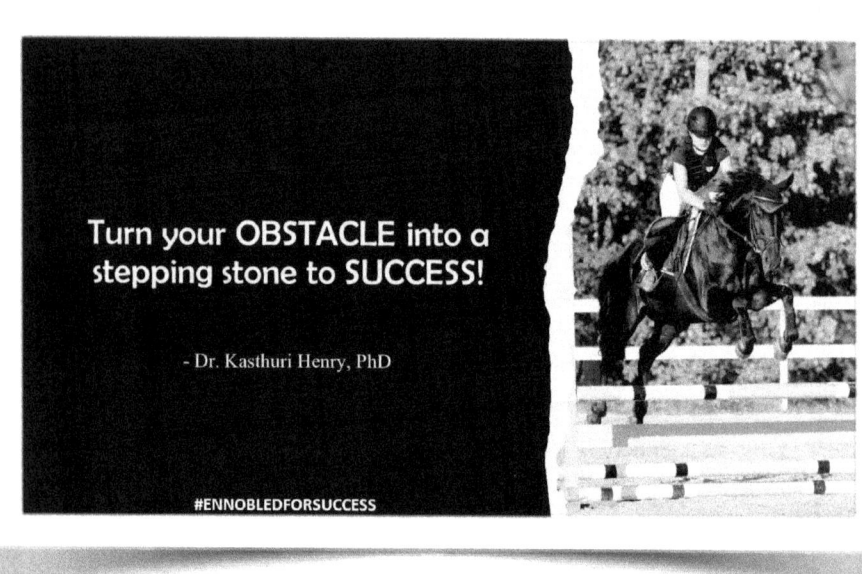

Weekly Reflection

Week ___

What happened this week?

How does this impact me?

Why am I grateful?

Weekly insight/reflection:

_____
_____
_____
_____
_____
_____

Weekly Reflection

Week ___

What happened this week?

How does this impact me?

Why am I grateful?

Weekly insight/reflection:

_____
_____
_____
_____
_____
_____

Weekly Reflection

Week ___

What happened this week?

How does this impact me?

Why am I grateful?

Weekly insight/reflection:

_____
_____
_____
_____
_____
_____

Wear your IDENTITY with PRIDE!

— Dr. Kasthuri Henry, PhD

#ENNOBLEDFORSUCCESS

Weekly Reflection

Week ___

What happened this week?

How does this impact me?

Why am I grateful?

Weekly insight/reflection:

_____
_____
_____
_____
_____
_____

 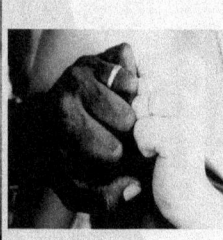

Beauty of our DIFFERENCES enhance our SHARED EXPERIENCES!

- Dr. Kasthuri Henry, PhD

#ENNOBLEDFORSUCCESS

Weekly Reflection

Week ___

What happened this week?

How does this impact me?

Why am I grateful?

Weekly insight/reflection:

_____
_____
_____
_____
_____
_____

Weekly Reflection

Week ___

What happened this week?

How does this impact me?

Why am I grateful?

Weekly insight/reflection:

_____

_____

_____

_____

_____

_____

Be VULNERABLE enough to be KIND.

Live with HUMILITY to LEARN.

Navigate life's CHALLANGES with GRACE.

- Dr. Kasthuri Henry, PhD

#ENNOBLEDFORSUCCESS

Weekly Reflection

Week ___

What happened this week?

How does this impact me?

Why am I grateful?

Weekly insight/reflection:

_____
_____
_____
_____
_____
_____

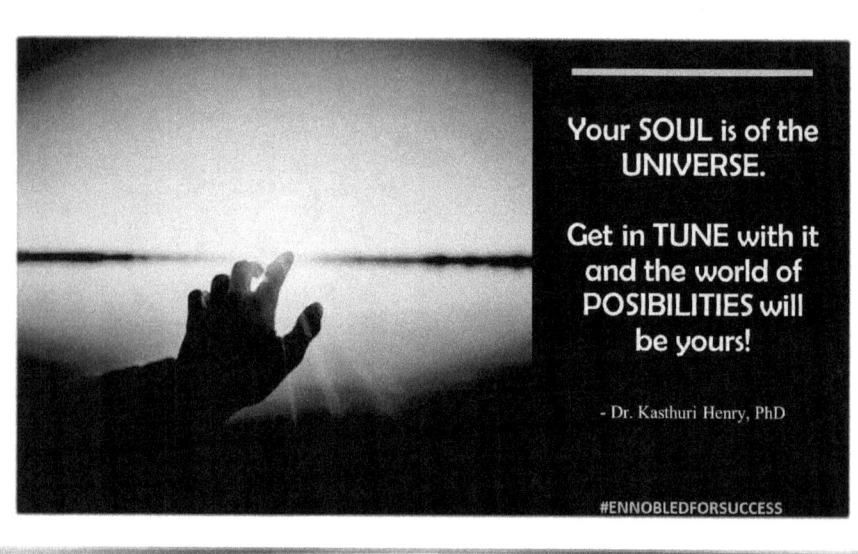

Weekly Reflection

Week ___

What happened this week?

How does this impact me?

Why am I grateful?

Weekly insight/reflection:

_____
_____
_____
_____
_____
_____

Weekly Reflection

Week ___

What happened this week?

How does this impact me?

Why am I grateful?

Weekly insight/reflection:

_____

_____

_____

_____

_____

_____

Weekly Reflection

Week ___

What happened this week?

How does this impact me?

Why am I grateful?

Weekly insight/reflection:

_____
_____
_____
_____
_____

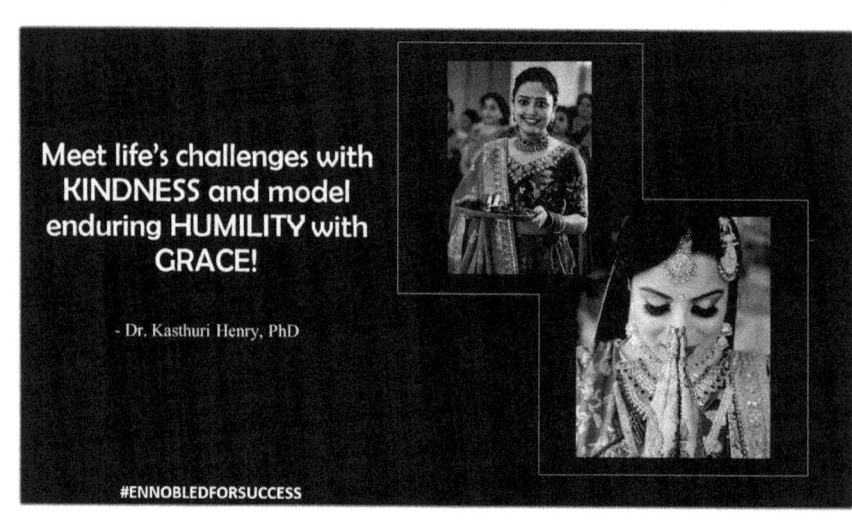

Weekly Reflection

Week ___

What happened this week?

How does this impact me?

Why am I grateful?

Weekly insight/reflection:

_____
_____
_____
_____
_____
_____

About the Author

Dr. Kasthuri Henry, PhD, is driven by her mission of **Building to Last and Ennobling for Success**. Her ability to understand the importance of first developing the *being,* and then bringing that authentic self to all the *doing,* makes her a sought-after member of Forbes' Coaches Council. She is a compassionate human being who believes everyone should have the opportunity to fulfill their life's purpose and live an authentic life fearlessly with the right to not be defined by a single story. She is an accomplished professional who trains organizations and coaches individuals around the world to grow with mindfulness, demonstrating good governance to balance the interest of the individual, organization, and society for sustained mutual prosperity. Dr. Kas has successfully led global transformation as a financial strategist, CFO, and change agent across Fortune-500 companies. As a graduate school professor at North Park University and Southern Illinois University, she continues to transform students representing the US military, US public safety and homeland security, private sector, and nonprofit sectors.

A centered approach to solving life's challenges is the theme of her weekly podcast, "**Unleash your Inner Goldilocks:** *How to get it just right!*"

Social Media links

Facebook: Facebook.com/DrKasHenry

LinkedIn: Linkedin.com/in/dr-kasthuri-henry-phd-mba-ctp-6-sigma-black-belt-2028b06/

Twitter: Twitter.com/DrKasthuri

Instagram: Instagram.com/henrykasthuri/

YouTube: Youtube.com/channel/UCtZZPdBCo_OTyccJLqEJc-A

www.ingramcontent.com/pod-product-compliance
Lightning Source LLC
LaVergne TN
LVHW051505070426
835507LV00022B/2928